Contents

Introduction 3

Step 1: Becoming a forex trader 9

Step 2: Understanding How the forex market works 12

Step 3: How to choose a broker and open a forex trading account
.... 28

How does a forex brokerage account work 28

The best forex broker for you 31

Choosing a forex broker 32

Step 4: 10 most volatile forex pairs to trade 49

Step5: Understanding pips, points and lots 60

Step6: Understanding FOREX terminologies: bid, ask and spread
.... 65

Step 7: Understanding how to use the technical analysis and fundamental analysis... 77

Technical analysis vs fundamental analysis 78

Understanding more about technical analysis 79

What is the basis of technical analysis 81

How is technical analysis used 82

Limitations of technical analysis 83

Step 8: How to send orders and different order types in forex .. 85

Market orders 86

Entry orders 87

Limit orders 88

Limit orders to open a trade 89

Limit orders to close a trade 90

Stop orders to open a trade 91

Stop orders to close a trade 91

How to place a forex order 93

Step 9: Get to know what traders use and how the think from a professional standpoint on 'IG' platform community 96

Summary 107

1

PROFITABLE FOREX TRADING

Steps to Achieving Profit; 10 + Most Volatile Forex Pairs to Trade

By Jim Peters

Introduction

Forex trading: Forex trading operates akin to conventional transactions, where an asset is acquired using a currency. In forex, the market price indicates the amount of one currency needed to buy another. For instance, the current market price of the GBP/USD pair reveals the quantity of US dollars necessary to purchase one pound. Each currency is assigned its unique code, facilitating swift identification within a pair. Below, I and my team have listed the codes for several widely traded currencies.

What does it signify to purchase or vend a currency duo?

Purchasing a currency pair suggests an anticipation of a price increase, indicating a strengthening of the base currency in relation to the quote currency. Conversely, selling a currency pair implies an expectation of a price decline, which would occur if the base currency depreciates against the quote currency.

For instance, opting to 'buy' the GBP/USD pair reflects confidence in the pound's potential to appreciate against the dollar, implying a greater need for dollars to acquire a single pound. Conversely, choosing to 'sell' this pair reflects a belief in the pound's potential depreciation against the dollar, signifying a reduced need for dollars to obtain a single pound.

Spread in forex: In forex trading, the spread refers to the variance between the buy and sell prices. For instance, the buy price could be quoted at 1.5427, while the sell price stands at 1.5424. To realize a profitable outcome, the market price must either surpass the buy price or dip below the sell price, contingent on whether you've taken a long or short position.

Margin and leverage in FX trading: Margin pertains to the preliminary deposit essential for initiating and upholding a leveraged stance. For instance, a transaction on EUR/USD might necessitate solely a 0.53% margin to be activated. Consequently, instead of mandating $200,000 to inaugurate a position, a mere $600 deposit would suffice.

Strength and weakness of taking position on currencies:

Traders anticipate movements in forex pairs to capitalize on fluctuations in the strength or weakness of one currency against another. When the price of a pair ascends, it signifies the base currency's reinforcement relative to the quote, whereas a decline suggests the base's depreciation against the quote.

This occurs because a rising price necessitates a greater amount of the quote currency to purchase a single unit of the base, while a falling price requires a reduced amount of the quote to obtain one unit of the base. Consequently, traders typically adopt a long position when the base currency is fortifying in relation to the quote currency or a short position when the base is depreciating.

Various forex trading styles, such as scalping, day trading, swing trading, and position trading, cater to different time horizons, be it short or long-term. Your preference for a particular style hinges on your outlook and objectives.

The forex market operates continuously 24 hours a day, facilitated by a vast network of banks and market makers engaged in perpetual currency exchanges. The primary trading sessions revolve around the US, Europe, and Asia, with the time disparities among these regions facilitating the round-the-clock availability of the forex market.

The allure of forex trading lies in its extended trading hours, providing traders with the flexibility to seize opportunities at any time. Additionally, we distinguish ourselves by offering weekend trading on select currency pairs, such as weekend GBP/USD, EUR/USD, and USD/JPY. This unique feature enables you to trade these pairs when others are unable to do so.

Hedging with forex: Hedging serves as a strategic approach to minimize risk exposure, accomplished by establishing positions that would yield profits in the event of declines in other positions, with the aim of mitigating losses to some extent. Currency correlations represent an effective method for hedging forex exposure. For instance, EUR/USD and GBP/USD exhibit positive correlation, meaning they typically move in tandem. Consequently, one might opt to short GBP/USD while holding a long position in EUR/USD to hedge against potential market downturns.

Step 1: Becoming a forex trader

There are various methods of engaging in forex trading, encompassing spot forex, forex futures, and currency options. When trading, you'll speculate on the direction of spot forex, futures, and options prices using a CFD account.

Spot forex trading enables you to trade forex pairs at their current market value without fixed expiration dates.

Forex or currency futures involve trading forex pairs at a predetermined price to be settled at a future date or within a range of future dates.

Forex or currency options involve trading contracts granting the holder the right, though not the obligation, to buy or sell a currency pair at a specified price if it surpasses that price within a predetermined time frame.

All these methods—spot, futures, and options—can be executed through FX CFDs, which are financial derivatives allowing you to speculate on price movements without owning the underlying asset.

Through FX CFDs, you can take positions on whether prices will rise or fall, offering flexibility and potential opportunities in the forex market. CFDs allow you to trade on margin, enabling you to amplify your trading capital and potentially increase your returns. However, it's important to be aware that trading CFDs also involves risks, including the possibility of losses exceeding your initial investment.

When trading spot forex, you can benefit from immediate execution at current market prices, allowing for quick entry and exit from trades. This flexibility can be advantageous for traders who prefer shorter-term trading strategies or who wish to capitalize on short-term market movements.

Forex futures provide the advantage of fixed expiration dates and standardized contract sizes, which can be useful for traders looking to hedge their currency exposure or engage in longer-term speculation. Futures contracts are traded on regulated exchanges, offering transparency and liquidity to market participants.

Currency options offer the flexibility of choosing whether or not to exercise the right to buy or sell a currency pair at a specified price within a predetermined time frame. Options can be used for hedging purposes or to capitalize on potential market volatility while limiting downside risk.

Overall, the availability of various forex trading instruments, including spot forex, futures, and options, allows traders to tailor their trading strategies to suit their preferences, risk tolerance, and investment objectives. By understanding the characteristics and advantages of each instrument, traders can make informed decisions and potentially enhance their trading outcomes in the dynamic forex market.

Step 2: Understanding How the forex market works

Participants: The forex market involves a wide range of participants, including central banks, commercial banks, hedge funds, institutional investors, retail traders, multinational corporations, and government institutions. Each participant contributes to the market's liquidity and plays a role in determining currency exchange rates.

Currency Pairs: There are numerous combinations available for selection, with some of the commonly favored ones including the euro versus the US dollar (EUR/USD), the US dollar versus the Japanese yen (USD/JPY), and the British pound versus the US dollar (GBP/USD). Currencies are traded in pairs, with each pair representing the exchange rate between two currencies. Examples are shown in the next page, the EUR/USD pair represents the exchange rate between the euro and the US dollar. In this pair, the euro is the base currency, and the US dollar is the quote currency. The exchange rate indicates how much of the quote currency is needed to purchase one unit of the base currency.

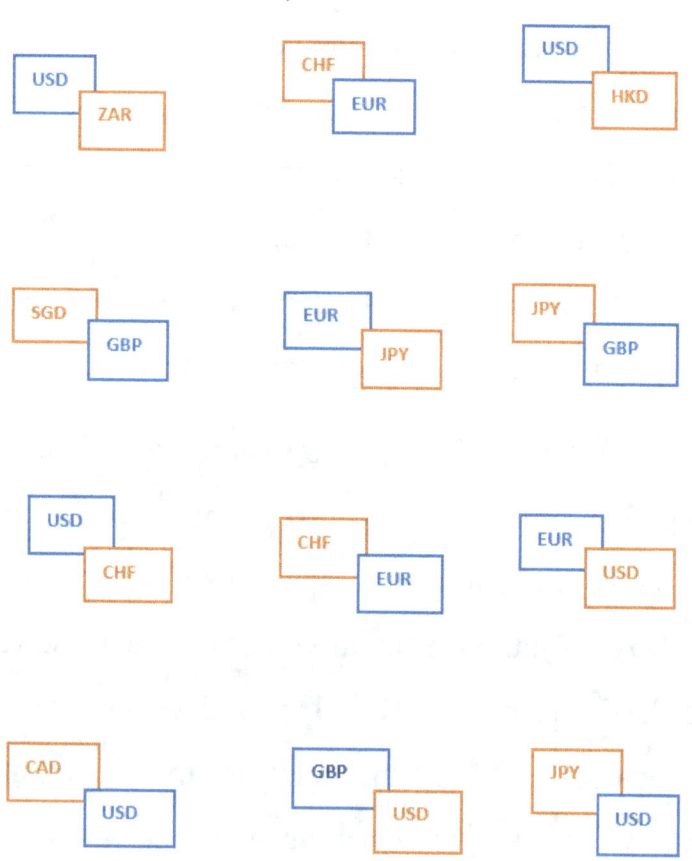

In a currency pair, the base currency is consistently positioned on the left, while the quote currency is consistently positioned on the right. The base currency always holds a value of one unit, while the quote currency reflects the current price of the pair indicating the amount of the quote currency needed to purchase one unit of the base currency.

1

Forex markets typically present their prices in pairs.

2

The price of a currency pair represents the amount of the quote currency required to purchase one unit of the base currency.

3

In forex trading, you're consistently purchasing one currency while simultaneously selling another.

EUR / USD = 1.24654

Base currency Quote currency

Let's look at a pip, in forex trading, a pip typically represents a one-unit movement in the fourth decimal place of a currency pair. For instance, if the GBP/USD pair shifts from $1.24654 to $1.24664, it has moved one pip. However, when trading JPY crosses, a pip denotes a change in the second decimal place. Additionally, a price variation at the fifth decimal place is referred to as a pipette in forex trading.

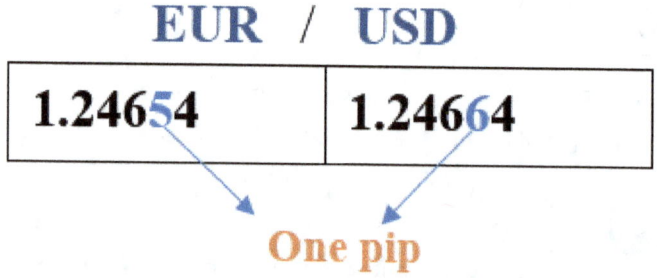

Currencies are also traded in lots, they are exchanged in lots, which are sets of currency utilized to standardize forex transactions. Given that forex price fluctuations are typically minor, lots tend to be sizable. For instance, a standard lot comprises 100,000 units of the base currency.

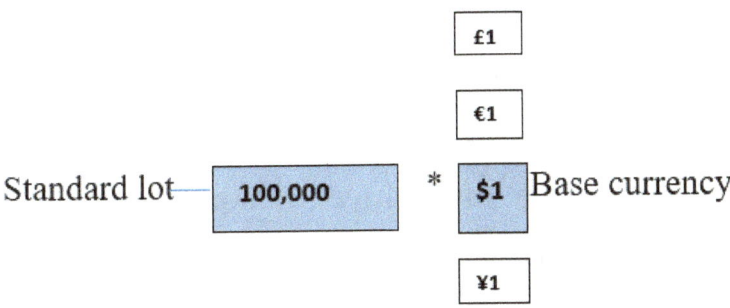

Market Structure: The forex market operates 24 hours a day, five days a week, across major financial centers worldwide. Trading occurs electronically over-the-counter (OTC), meaning there is no centralized exchange. Instead, transactions are conducted through a network of banks, brokers, and electronic trading platforms. The major trading centers include London, New York, Tokyo, Sydney, and Frankfurt.

Price Determination: Exchange rates in the forex market are determined by supply and demand dynamics. Various factors influence supply and demand, including economic indicators (e.g., GDP growth, inflation, employment data), central bank policies, geopolitical events, and market sentiment. For example, if there is increased demand for the US dollar due to positive economic data or a hawkish monetary policy statement from the Federal Reserve, the value of the dollar may appreciate against other currencies.

Bid and Ask Prices: In every currency pair, there are two prices: the bid price and the ask price. The bid price is the price at which buyers are willing to purchase the base currency, while the ask price is the price at which sellers are willing to sell the base currency. The difference between the bid and ask prices is known as the spread. For example, if the bid price for EUR/USD is 1.2000, and the ask price is 1.2005, the spread is 5 pips.

Leverage and Margin: Forex trading often involves the use of leverage, which allows traders to control larger positions with a relatively small amount of capital. Leverage amplifies both potential profits and losses. Traders must maintain a margin account with their broker to access leverage. For example, with a leverage ratio of 1:50, a trader can control a position worth $50,000 with a margin of $1,000.

Let's consider a live example of trading the EUR/USD pair. Suppose the current exchange rate for EUR/USD is 1.2050. A trader believes that the euro will strengthen against the US dollar and decides to buy 100,000 euros. The trader enters a long (buy) position at 1.2050. If the exchange rate later rises to 1.2100, the trader can close the position by selling 100,000 euros at the new exchange rate. The trader's profit would be the difference between the buy and sell prices, multiplied by the position size (100,000 euros), minus any trading costs such as spreads and commissions.

Market Liquidity: Liquidity refers to the ease with which an asset can be bought or sold without causing significant price changes. The forex market is known for its high liquidity, meaning that traders can enter and exit positions with minimal slippage, even when dealing with large volumes of currency. High liquidity ensures that there is always a counterparty available to take the other side of a trade, contributing to the market's efficiency.

Market Orders and Order Types: Traders can execute trades in the forex market using various order types, including market orders, limit orders, stop orders, and contingent orders. A market order is an instruction to buy or sell a currency pair at the current market price. A limit order is an instruction to buy or sell a currency pair at a specified price or better. A stop order is an instruction to buy or sell a currency pair once the market reaches a specified price level, known as the stop price. Contingent orders, such as OCO (One Cancels the Other) and OTO (One Triggers the Other), allow traders to set up multiple orders simultaneously, with one order triggering the execution of another.

Currency Volatility: Volatility refers to the degree of variation in the price of a currency pair over time. Currency volatility can be influenced by factors such as economic data releases, geopolitical events, central bank announcements, and market sentiment. Higher volatility can present trading opportunities for profit but also increases the risk of significant losses. Traders should be aware of currency volatility and adjust their trading strategies and risk management accordingly.

Over-the-Counter (OTC) Trading: The forex market operates over-the-counter, meaning that trades are executed directly between counterparties without a centralized exchange. This decentralized structure allows for flexibility and accessibility but also requires traders to conduct due diligence when selecting brokers and counterparties. Unlike centralized exchanges, there is no single price for a currency pair in the forex market. Instead, prices may vary slightly between different brokers and liquidity providers.

Market Sentiment and News Trading: Market sentiment refers to the overall attitude of traders and investors towards a particular currency pair or the forex market as a whole. Market sentiment can be influenced by factors such as economic data releases, geopolitical events, and news headlines. Traders often analyze market sentiment indicators, such as the Commitments of Traders (COT) report, to gauge market sentiment and identify potential trading opportunities. News trading involves trading significant news events, such as central bank announcements or geopolitical based on the immediate market reaction to developments.

Regulation and Oversight: The forex market is subject to regulation and oversight in many jurisdictions to ensure fair and transparent trading practices and protect investors. Regulatory bodies such as the Commodity Futures Trading

Commission (CFTC) in the United States, the Financial Conduct Authority (FCA) in the United Kingdom, and the Australian Securities and Investments Commission (ASIC) in Australia enforce regulations and oversee forex brokers and other market participants. Regulation helps maintain market integrity, prevent fraud and market manipulation, and safeguard traders' interests.

Currency Crosses and Exotic Pairs: While major currency pairs involve currencies paired with the US dollar (e.g., EUR/USD, GBP/USD), traders also deal with currency crosses and exotic pairs. Currency crosses involve pairs that do not include the US dollar (e.g., EUR/GBP, AUD/JPY), while exotic pairs involve currencies from emerging or smaller economies (e.g., USD/TRY, EUR/SEK). Trading these pairs allows traders to diversify their exposure and take advantage of specific currency relationships.

Central Bank Interventions: Central banks occasionally intervene in the forex market to stabilize their currencies or achieve specific policy objectives. Central bank interventions can take various forms, such as direct currency purchases or sales, verbal interventions (e.g., statements from central bank officials), and changes in monetary policy. These interventions can have a significant impact on currency prices and may influence traders' behavior and market sentiment.

Algorithmic Trading and High-Frequency Trading (HFT): Algorithmic trading and high-frequency trading (HFT) have become increasingly prevalent in the forex market. Algorithmic trading involves the use of computer algorithms to execute trades automatically based on predefined criteria, such as price movements, technical indicators, or news events. HFT refers to the use of sophisticated algorithms and high-speed connections to execute large volumes of trades in fractions of a second.

These automated trading strategies contribute to market liquidity but can also lead to increased market volatility and rapid price fluctuations.

Role of Economic Calendar: Economic calendars are essential tools for forex traders as they provide information about upcoming economic events, data releases, central bank meetings, and other significant events that may impact currency prices. Traders use economic calendars to plan their trading activities, anticipate potential market movements, and adjust their trading strategies accordingly. Key events to watch include interest rate decisions, GDP releases, inflation reports, employment data, and speeches by central bank officials.

Risk Factors in Forex Trading: Forex trading involves various risks that traders should be aware of, including market risk, liquidity risk, leverage risk, counterparty risk, and geopolitical risk. Market risk arises from fluctuations in currency prices, while liquidity risk relates to the possibility of encountering difficulty in executing trades at desired prices. Leverage risk refers to the potential for amplified losses due to trading on margin, while counterparty risk pertains to the risk of default by trading counterparties. Geopolitical risk arises from political instability, conflicts, or other geopolitical events that can impact currency values.

Psychology of Trading: The psychology of trading plays a crucial role in forex trading success. Emotions such as fear, greed, and overconfidence can cloud judgment and lead to irrational decision-making. Successful traders maintain discipline, patience, and emotional control, adhere to their trading plans, and manage risk effectively. Developing a mindset focused on continuous learning, resilience, and adaptability is essential for navigating the challenges of forex trading and achieving long-term success.

Continuous Learning and Improvement: Forex trading is a dynamic and ever-evolving field, requiring traders to stay informed about market developments, technological advancements, and regulatory changes. Continuous learning and improvement are essential for staying competitive and adapting to changing market conditions. Traders can enhance their skills and knowledge through educational resources, trading courses, books, seminars, webinars, and mentorship programs. Additionally, keeping a trading journal, analyzing past trades, and seeking feedback from experienced traders can help identify strengths, weaknesses, and areas for improvement.

Step 3: How to choose a broker and open a forex trading account

A forex broker is a person or entity that enables traders to engage in the purchase and sale of foreign currencies. "IG" is an example of a trusted forex broker. Their platform serves as an intermediary, allowing you to speculate on the value of a forex pair without the need to physically purchase any currencies.

How does a forex brokerage account work

Forex brokerage accounts operate with some variation depending on the region of trading, and the specifics will be determined by the broker you select. strive to ensure simplicity in your forex account setups.

- A forex brokerage account can function as either an investment account, where you directly purchase currencies and own them outright, or as a trading account, where you speculate on currency values in the market. With us, you'd open a CFD trading account, which we'll elaborate on further.

- Given that the forex market operates non-stop, a reputable forex brokerage should offer you access to foreign exchange trading 24 hours a day, five days a week. With "IG", you can trade forex from 5 am Monday to 6 am Saturday (UTC+8). This extensive trading availability is possible due to forex transactions being conducted over the counter (OTC), rather than through a central exchange.

- Once your account is set up, you'll need to select a currency pair to trade. With them, you have access to over 80 currency pairs, ranging from major pairs like GBP/USD and EUR/USD to more minor and exotic pairs like USD/ZAR or AUD/CNH.

- Forex trades are conducted in lots, which are standardized batch sizes of currency pairs used for speculation. For instance, a standard lot consists of 100,000 units of the base currency, although smaller denominations are also available. Before initiating trades, it's essential to determine the lot size and amount you're comfortable investing.

- Remember, when trading forex, it's not just about the lot sizes. Both your position size and the instrument's price must be considered in calculating costs. Additionally, other fees and charges may be applicable.
- In a forex brokerage account, you're in control, not a fund manager. Therefore, you'll need to monitor and analyze currency market movements closely, keeping a watchful eye on any open positions and setting alerts to avoid missing significant market shifts.

For this reason, it's crucial to implement a sound risk management strategy to maximize profit potential and minimize the likelihood of losses.

The best forex broker for you

Choosing the ideal forex broker hinges on your unique trading style and aspirations. Regardless of your preferences, the perfect forex broker should offer:

- Trading hours aligned with your preferred trading times, taking into account your chosen currency pair. "IG" platform provides 24/5 trading, along with weekend trading hours.

- A comprehensive suite of platforms tailored to meet your requirements. They offer a range of options, including our classic platform, mobile app, Pro-Real-Time, L2 Dealer, and MT4.

- Transparent fee structures with no hidden charges. With them, you'll enjoy free deposits and withdrawals.

Ultimately, determining the right forex brokerage necessitates trial and error. Experimenting with various platforms is essential to pinpointing the one that complements your specific FX strategy.

Choosing a forex broker

The forex market is the biggest, most liquid (and often the most volatile) market in the world – so you really want a forex broker you can rely on. Here are nine factors to consider when choosing a foreign exchange broker:

1. Trading hours
2. Amount of forex markets available
3. Educational tools available
4. Customer service
5. Regulatory compliance
6. Leverage and margin amounts
7. Deposits and withdrawals
8. Spread and commission rate
9. Trading platforms

Trading hours

The forex market operates incessantly, earning its distinction as the largest and most liquid market globally. Every day, individuals, corporations, and financial institutions engage in forex transactions amounting to trillions of dollars.

While major forex hubs like London, New York, Tokyo, and Sydney serve as focal points, currency exchanges occur within these locales round the clock, involving currencies from nations spanning diverse time zones. This global dynamic renders forex a 24-hour market with international reach.

Given this pervasive nature of forex trading, it becomes imperative to select a forex broker capable of providing extensive trading hours. For instance, consider a trader in the UK participating in USD/AUD trades; they must account for the fact that New York trading commences at 12 pm UK time, while Australia's trading activities initiate at 9 pm local time.

You have the opportunity to engage in forex trading with "IG" round the clock, five days a week. Their weekend trading hours extend from 12 pm on Saturday to 4:40 am on Monday (UTC +8). Additionally, they provide weekend trading options for major currency pairs such as GBP/USD, EUR/USD, and USD/JPY.

Amount of forex markets available

As a forex trader, it's not only crucial to have access to extensive trading hours but also to a diverse range of currency pairs to align with your unique trading style and strategy. Each currency pair possesses distinct characteristics, including varying levels of volatility and potential opportunities.

"IG" offers over 80 of the world's most popular currency pairs for trading, encompassing:

- Major pairs such as GBP/USD, EUR/USD, GBP/EUR, and USD/JPY

- Minor pairs including CAD/CHF, USD/ZAR, and SGB/JPY

- Emerging currency pairs like USD/CNH and AUD/CNH

- Exotic pairs such as EUR/CZK, TRY/JPY, and USD/MXN

Furthermore, they provide different trading options for these currencies, allowing you to engage in real-time trading (known as spot trading) or to take longer-term futures positions via FX options. This diversity empowers you to tailor your trading approach to suit your preferences and objectives effectively.

Educational tools available

Selecting an online broker that provides abundant training materials and learning resources on forex can be advantageous. Enhancing your understanding of FX trading directly correlates with your potential for success in trading endeavors, enabling you to capitalize on profit opportunities while mitigating risks.

With "IG Academy", you have the opportunity to enhance your trading knowledge and skills through a range of courses offered at your own pace, entirely free of charge. Following your learning, you can apply your newfound skills by practicing with a free "IG" demo trading account, which includes $20,000 in virtual funds for experimentation before venturing into live forex trading.

Additionally, they offer strategy tips, news and analysis articles, and insights from our in-house analysts, equipping you with valuable information to comprehend ongoing developments in the forex market effectively.

Customer service

Even with a solid trading strategy, there will be occasions when you require assistance. Opting for an online trading broker with a robust platform is essential, but equally vital is their capacity to support you when queries arise.

This aspect becomes particularly critical for forex traders, given the round-the-clock nature of trading and the prevalence of platforms based in different time zones. It's essential to assess the availability of customer support and their responsiveness to inquiries, especially during non-traditional trading hours.

"IG" customer support is accessible via phone or email around the clock, with the exception of the period from 4 am to 6 pm on Saturdays (UTC+8). This tailored approach is designed to cater to the needs of forex traders, many of whom engage in trading outside regular office hours and rely on platforms like Twitter(X) for FX trading insights.

Furthermore, if you're a novice forex trader considering trading with them, their client services team is available to provide a personalized walkthrough of our platform during the account setup process. This individualized assistance ensures a seamless onboarding experience for beginners.

Regulatory compliance

When selecting a broker, you should consider to adhere to their regulatory standards. Entrusting your forex transactions to a broker entail placing your trust in their integrity and compliance with legal requirements.

"IG" platform stands as a reputable entity subject to regulation by multiple global regulatory bodies, including the FCA, BaFin, MAS, ASIC, NFA, and CFTC. These regulatory authorities impose stringent requirements that dictate the operational conduct of brokers, ensuring transparency and accountability in their dealings. Furthermore, regulated firms are mandated to segregate client funds from their own accounts, safeguarding client assets in the event of insolvency.

"IG" International Limited holds licenses from the Bermuda Monetary Authority (BMA) to conduct investment business and digital asset business. This regulatory oversight underscores the commitment to client protection and financial integrity.

By adhering to regulatory standards and implementing measures such as segregating client funds, "IG" Group provides reassurance that client funds are ringfenced and protected, offering peace of mind to traders.

Leverage and margin amounts

Understanding leverage and margin amounts is fundamental to trading certain financial instruments. Essentially, it involves borrowing a portion of your position size from your broker. When initiating a forex trade, you contribute a percentage of its value, known as margin, while the broker covers the remainder.

This arrangement allows you to open a trade with only a fraction of the position's actual size, yet both profits and losses are calculated based on the trade's full value. Consequently, the potential gains or losses can far exceed the initial margin amount.

The ratio of your total exposure to the margin deposited is termed the leverage ratio. To illustrate, suppose you wish to purchase 1000 shares of a company at a share price of 100 cents. In a conventional trade, you'd need to pay the full value of $1000 upfront. However, with leverage, you may only need to deposit a fraction, say 20%, or $200, to open the position.

If the share price rises by 40 cents, resulting in a profit of $400, you effectively double your initial margin. Conversely, if the share price falls by the same amount, you incur a $400 loss, equivalent to twice your initial margin.

The leverage ratio offered by your forex broker is crucial, as it determines the extent to which you can amplify your trading position with minimal capital. While high leverage ratios can potentially magnify profits, they also entail substantial risks, with losses exceeding your position size. Therefore, exercising caution when utilizing leverage is paramount to safeguarding your trading strategy. It's worth noting that their platform provides negative balance protection, ensuring that you cannot lose more than the equity available in your account. In the event of a negative balance, they cover the deficit at no cost to you.

For further insights, here are specific margin and leverage details for some of our most popular currency pairs:

FX pair	Retail margin	Leverage equivalent	Value per point (standard*)
EUR/USD	0.50%	1:200	$10
GBP/USD	0.50%	1:200	$10
EUR/GBP	0.50%	1:200	£10
AUD/USD	0.50%	1:200	$10
USD/CAD	0.50%	1:200	C$10
USD/JPY	0.50%	1:200	HKD10

Deposits and withdrawals

When considering different forex brokers, it's crucial to be aware of any additional fees associated with trading, as they can impact your overall trading experience significantly. These fees often come into play during various stages, including:

- Making your initial deposit to commence forex trading

- Depositing funds into your account thereafter

- Withdrawing profits as funds

With "IG" platform, there is no minimum deposit amount required for bank transfers, although deposits via credit or debit card may incur a fee. Moreover, there's no obligation to fund your account immediately upon setup, a requirement imposed by some other brokers. They strive to streamline the deposit process, offering multiple payment options such as credit card, debit card, and bank transfer. Additionally, you may opt to transfer funds from a Wise account, although we advise you to review associated costs independently as we are not affiliated with Wise.

Credit card payments are processed instantly, while bank transfers may take up to three working days.

In the interim, you can upload proof of payment to initiate trading promptly.

When it comes to withdrawing funds, there are no fees involved with their platform. You can withdraw funds via wire transfer or most credit/debit cards, with card withdrawals typically clearing within two to five bank working days. Bank transfer withdrawals may take one to three working days to clear. However, withdrawals requiring currency conversion at the prevailing spot rate incur a conversion charge of 0.5%. These requests are handled manually and may entail longer processing times. Please note that while there is no minimum deposit amount for bank transfers, the minimum for card payments is $300, as indicated on the payment screen. In addition to fee considerations, it's essential to evaluate the trading platforms offered by different brokers to ensure they align with your trading needs and preferences.

Spread and commission rate

The cost of opening a position in forex trading extends beyond the margin rate, encompassing another component known as 'the spread.' Unlike traditional trading setups, you won't incur any commission charges with "IG"; however, you will encounter spreads. The spread refers to the disparity between the buy and sell prices at the onset of a forex trade. Typically, they impose their own spread on top of the market spread, serving as their fee for facilitating the trade. These spread charges are applicable to CFD trades involving forex.

The magnitude of the spread is predominantly influenced by the prevailing economic conditions in the market. In times of heightened volatility, the spread widens to mitigate the associated risks. While they endeavor to maintain our minimum spread under normal market conditions, it may expand when market prices fluctuate significantly.

Here are the minimum spread amounts for some of the most sought-after FX pairs:

FX pair	Minimum spread amount
EUR/USD	0.6
GBP/USD	0.9
AUD/USD	0.6
EUR/GBP	0.9
USD/CAD	1.3
EUR/JPY	1.5
USD/CHF	1.5

Trading platforms

While all forex brokers offer a trading platform for executing trades, not all platforms are alike, and the selection of platforms can vary among brokers.

At "IG" brokerage, they boast award-winning trading platforms and mobile apps for seamless trading experiences. They offer a diverse range of platforms for our clients to choose from. In addition to their user-friendly mobile platform and app, traders can access Pro-Real-Time and our DMA (direct market access) platform L2 Dealer. Moreover, we provide Meta-Trader 4 (MT4), a globally recognized third-party platform widely utilized in the industry.

How to start forex trading with "IG"

Follow these four steps:

1. Click on this link below or copy it to your browser to register on "IG" platform
https://www.ig.com/en/application-form
2. Fill in a form; In this section, they'll inquire about your trading expertise to tailor the experience to your needs.
3. Upon completion, verification will swiftly follow.
4. Subsequently, you can fund your account and commence trading.

Step 4: 10 most volatile forex pairs to trade

Before delving into pips, points and lots, let's first grasp how volatility is gauged. Volatility serves as a metric for assessing the extent of price fluctuations within a specific financial market. In this discourse, we will utilize the average 30-day realized volatility observed over the past three years to gauge volatility, offering us a historical context regarding the price movements of currency pairs.

It's worth emphasizing that volatility can exhibit an inverse correlation with liquidity. When a market experiences heightened volatility, its liquidity tends to diminish. This phenomenon occurs because elevated volatility introduces uncertainty and unpredictability into the market, prompting market makers to widen their bid-ask spreads. Furthermore, volatility may fluctuate throughout the trading day, influenced by the opening and closing of different markets. Typically, markets are most liquid during the London session and least liquid preceding the Japan session.

1. USD/SGD - Volatility: 3.9%

Among the top 10 currency pairs, USD/SGD stands out as the least volatile, averaging under 4% over recent years. This minor pair has exhibited relatively limited price movements, rendering it less appealing for swing traders seeking rapid price fluctuations.

2. EUR/USD - Volatility: 6.6%

In recent years, the euro has displayed decreased volatility, averaging around 6.6% against the US dollar. Despite EUR/USD witnessing a decline of approximately 10% in its value and even reaching parity in 2022, it has not encountered significant short-term price fluctuations.

3. USD/CHF - Volatility: 6.7%

Over the past three years, the Swiss franc has maintained stability relative to the USD, although USD/CHF did briefly reach parity before declining by 1000 pips below the 0.9000 level. This relatively low volatility could be beneficial for certain traders, given that the pair is often considered a safe-haven currency in times of market uncertainty.

4. USD/CAD - Volatility: 6.1%

The Canadian dollar has demonstrated less volatility against the USD, largely due to the strong economic connections between the United States and Canada. However, fluctuations in crude oil prices, given Canada's significant oil exports, can introduce volatility to the commodity currency.

5. GBP/USD - Volatility: 7.7%

The British Pound exhibits comparatively lower volatility in comparison to the aforementioned pairs, with an average volatility of 7.7% against the US dollar over the past three years. Although it has undergone a notable decline, its range has been relatively narrow, spanning 25% from 1.4000 to 1.0500.

6. USD/JPY - Volatility: 7.6%

Despite experiencing a decline of over 40% in value against the US dollar, the Japanese yen has displayed relatively lower volatility, just above 7%. This is attributed to the fact that while the currency pair has reached historical extremes over time, it has not witnessed significant short-term percentage fluctuations.

7. USD/ZAR - Volatility: 12.9%

In recent years, the South African rand has demonstrated high volatility, averaging nearly 13% over the past three years. Additionally, it has encountered substantial price fluctuations, declining by over 20% against the US dollar and exhibiting a significant high-to-low range of almost 50%.

8. NZD/USD - Volatility: 9.5%

The New Zealand dollar, closely linked to the Australian economy, has shown comparable volatility to the AUD, averaging 9.5% over the past three years.

9. USD/MXN - Volatility: 9.2%

The US dollar has experienced notable fluctuations against the Mexican peso, appreciating by 13% in recent years. It has fluctuated between highs of 22.000 and lows below 17.000, rendering it appealing to traders in search of volatility.

10. AUD/USD - Volatility: 9.6%

The Australian dollar has displayed considerable volatility, depreciating by 12% in the past three years. Its trading range has spanned from historical lows near 0.6000 to highs nearing 0.8000. Although traditionally considered a commodity currency due to Australia's gold production, the AUD has shown correlation with stocks and China's economic performance in recent times.

Step5: Understanding pips, points and lots

In forex trading, a pip serves as a crucial metric for measuring price movements between two currencies. Derived from "point in percentage," a pip represents the smallest standardized increment by which a currency quote can fluctuate. Traders utilize pips to gauge the spread between bid and ask prices of currency pairs and to assess the profit or loss incurred by their positions.

Typically, major currencies delineate a pip as the fourth decimal place, equating to a one pip change of 0.0001. However, exceptions exist, such as with the Japanese Yen, where a pip is determined by the second digit after the decimal point. Despite conventionally being associated with the second or fourth decimal place, it's common to encounter an additional decimal representing a fraction of a pip.

The spread of a currency pair can be expressed in pips, offering insight into market price movements. Essentially, a pip signifies the equivalent of a singular "point" of movement. While at "IG" they quantify currency fluctuations in pips for CFD trades, we refer to them as points.

Examples of pips

Let's examine the EUR/USD currency pair. If the market shifts from 1.1300 to 1.1302, this uptick of 0.0002 denotes a single pip movement.

Suppose you initiated a long position on EUR/USD, and the market surged from 1.1800 to 1.1890. In this scenario, you would have gained 90 pips and capitalized on the upward trend. Conversely, if the market trended against you, dropping from 1.1800 to 1.1770, resulting in a decline of 90 pips, your position would have incurred a loss.

Now, consider the USD/JPY currency pair. A shift from 140.03 to 140.04 signifies a one-pip movement.

Assume you opted for a long position on the pair, and the price escalated from 140.00 to 140.07. This indicates an advancement of seven pips, signaling a profitable outcome for your position.

Lot in forex

Understanding the concept of a forex lot is essential for trading currency pairs effectively. A lot serves as a standardized unit of measurement for trade size, facilitating the trading of small currency value changes, known as pips, which are typically represented in the fourth decimal place.

The value of a lot is determined by regulatory bodies or exchanges, ensuring uniformity in trade sizes and providing traders with clarity regarding their position sizes. Lots come in various sizes –

standard, mini, micro, and nano – offering traders flexibility in managing their exposure to the market.

To illustrate, consider a company selling a set of cosmetics in standard pack of 3 and 6 packages. Similarly, in forex trading, you cannot purchase individual units of currency; instead, you transact in lots of standardized sizes. For instance, you may trade 100,000 units of the base currency GBP in a standard lot or 1000 units in a micro lot.

The lot size in forex depends on whether you are trading standard, mini, micro, or nano lots, each serving as a standardized unit for measuring currency value changes. Your trading platform typically specifies the available lot sizes, and you can calculate your position size by multiplying the lot size by the number of lots you wish to trade.

With "IG", you have the flexibility to trade standard or micro lots using CFDs, allowing you to adjust your position size according to your risk tolerance. The monetary value of a one-pip movement varies based on the lot size, with larger lot sizes magnifying both profits and losses. For example, for the EURUSD currency pair:

- A standard lot equals $10 per one-pip movement

- A mini lot equals $1 per one-pip movement

- A micro lot equals $0.10 per one-pip movement

- A nano lot equals $0.01 per one-pip movement

Choosing the appropriate lot size involves considering your risk tolerance and the amount of leverage you intend to use, as larger lot sizes require greater capital outlay and amplify pip movement effects.

Step6: Understanding FOREX terminologies: bid, ask and spread

Understanding the bid-ask spread is essential for any forex trader, as it represents one of the primary costs associated with trading. Often overlooked by novice traders, the bid-ask spread significantly influences the overall cost of executing trades. In this article, I and my team will explore the intricacies of the bid-ask spread, including its calculation, factors influencing its size, and strategies to mitigate its impact on your trading activities. The bid-ask spread refers to the difference between the highest price a buyer is willing to pay (bid price) and the lowest price a seller is willing to accept (ask price) for a particular asset, such as a currency pair in forex trading. This spread effectively represents the cost of executing a trade and serves as compensation for the market maker facilitating the transaction.

The calculation of the bid-ask spread is straightforward: it is simply the difference between the ask price and the bid price. For example, if the current ask price for a currency pair is 1.2000 and the bid price is 1.1990, then the bid-ask spread would be 0.0010, or 10 pips.

Several factors influence the size of the bid-ask spread, including market liquidity, trading volume, and market volatility. Generally, more liquid markets with higher trading volumes tend to have narrower spreads, while less liquid markets with lower volumes may exhibit wider spreads. Additionally, during periods of high volatility or low liquidity, spreads typically widen as market makers adjust prices to manage risk.

To mitigate the impact of the bid-ask spread on your trading costs, consider employing strategies such as trading during times of high liquidity, avoiding trading during periods of extreme volatility, and selecting currency pairs with narrower spreads.

Additionally, utilizing limit orders to enter and exit trades can help ensure that you execute at desired price levels, minimizing slippage and reducing trading costs associated with wider spreads.

By understanding the dynamics of the bid-ask spread and implementing effective trading strategies, you can better manage your trading costs and improve your overall trading performance in the forex market.

What is the bid-ask spread

Let's make more insight, at its core, the bid-ask spread signifies the disparity between the ask price, which denotes the lowest price a seller is willing to accept for an asset, and the bid price, which represents the highest price a buyer is willing to pay for the same asset. Essentially, it delineates the cost of executing a trade. Despite the allure of zero-commission trading offered by some stock or forex brokers, the bid-ask spread persists as an inherent transaction expense, as the true market price resides at the midpoint between these two prices. Moreover, ancillary expenses like margin requirements or buying power further contribute to the overall expenditure associated with your trading endeavors. Understanding and factoring in these costs is crucial for accurately assessing the financial implications of your trades.

Spreads initiate from a mere 0.8 pips on EUR/USD.

Conduct in-depth analysis of market fluctuations using "IG" comprehensive array of charts.

Engage in speculative trading across various platforms, including mobile accessibility.

How it is calculated

Determining the bid-ask spread is a relatively simple process. You just subtract the bid price from the ask price to find the spread. For instance, if a stock has a bid price of $10.05 and an ask price of $10.06, the spread would be one penny. This same method applies to assets such as Forex, where you deduct the bid price from the ask price to gauge the spread.

Moreover, the size of your trade and the specific market you're engaged in also influence the spread cost. For example, if you're trading one share of stock with a one-penny spread, the cost would amount to one penny. However, if you're trading a hundred shares, the cost would escalate to $1.00. As your trade size increases, the impact of the spread cost becomes more pronounced. This principle extends to various markets, including derivatives like options and futures, each with their own ticks and spreads.

These spreads are not static and can fluctuate based on market conditions and liquidity. During times of high volatility or low liquidity, spreads tend to widen, increasing the cost of trading. This variability underscores the importance of closely monitoring market conditions and understanding how they can affect trading costs. Additionally, traders should consider factors like the time of day and economic events, as these can also influence spread sizes. By staying informed and adapting their strategies accordingly, traders can better navigate the dynamic landscape of bid-ask spreads in various markets.

Factors that affect the size of a spread

Volatility: it is an influential factor shaping the bid-ask spread. Markets experiencing higher volatility, especially during times of uncertainty or significant events such as economic crises or central bank announcements, often witness wider spreads. This occurs because heightened volatility leads to rapid price fluctuations, prompting market makers to widen spreads to mitigate risk.

Liquidity: plays a crucial role in determining the bid-ask spread across various assets. In markets with high liquidity, characterized by significant trading volumes and numerous participants, spreads tend to be narrower. This phenomenon occurs because market makers can efficiently match trades due to the abundance of buy and sell orders. For instance, widely traded stocks like Apple or Microsoft boast tighter spreads compared to less liquid stocks. Similarly, in Forex trading, currency pairs with substantial trading volumes and participant activity, such as EUR/USD, typically exhibit narrower spreads than those with lower liquidity, like USD/ZAR. It's essential to note that liquidity can fluctuate throughout the day, influencing optimal trading times in the forex market.

Quote currency: Moreover, the choice of quote currency in forex pairs can impact spread costs. Unlike assets like stocks or commodities priced in U.S. dollars, forex pairs are denominated in various currencies. Consequently, the value per pip in a forex pair is determined by the quote currency. For instance, in the USD/JPY pair, where the quote currency is the Japanese yen, the value per pip is

1,000 yen, translating to different amounts in U.S. dollars based on prevailing exchange rates.

This variability underscores the importance of understanding the dynamics of liquidity, volatility, and quote currencies when assessing spread costs in different markets. By considering these factors, traders can make informed decisions and navigate the intricacies of bid-ask spreads more effectively to optimize their trading strategies.

How to see the bid-ask spread

"IG" platform conveniently displays the spread between the "Buy" and "Sell" buttons, providing traders with essential information for decision-making. This numerical value, expressed in pips, usually extends to the fourth decimal place (0.0001), offering clarity and precision in assessing trading costs.

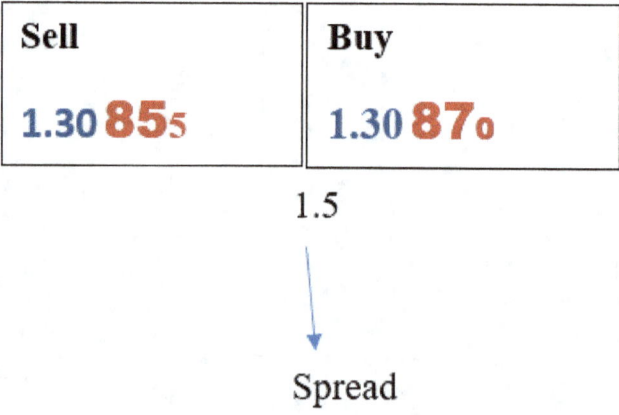

The bid-ask spread cost directly influences your profit and loss (P&L) statement. Whenever you execute a trade, whether buying or selling an asset with a particular spread, the incurred cost is subtracted from your P&L. For instance, engaging in a market transaction with a spread of one-and-a-half pips would result in a negative $15 reflected in your P&L. This principle remains consistent across various asset classes, such as stocks, where the bid-ask spread plays a crucial role in determining your potential gains or losses.

How to mitigate spread costs

Traders can minimize high spread costs by taking into account the factors influencing the spread. Opting for highly liquid pairs during active market hours often yields better prices. Limit orders offer traders the ability to set the desired price level for opening a position and can help mitigate the impact on a trade's profit or loss (P/L). By placing a limit order slightly beyond the current spread, traders may quickly secure a fill at the designated price. For buying, this entails setting a limit order below the market price, and conversely for selling. However, it's crucial to monitor limit orders closely as they may not always be executed.

It's worth noting that spreads vary across different markets. Markets with higher liquidity and lower volatility typically exhibit tighter spreads. For example, established Forex pairs like euro-dollar and dollar-yen tend to have tighter average spreads due to their longevity, higher trading volumes, and broader participation.

In summary, the bid-ask spread significantly impacts the overall cost of trading. Familiarizing oneself with its mechanics and its effects on various markets is pivotal for making well-informed investment choices. By considering factors such as liquidity, volatility, and trade size, traders can effectively manage spread costs and refine their trading approach.

Step 7: Understanding how to use the technical analysis and fundamental analysis

Technical analysis involves forecasting the future price movement of a market by analyzing historical chart patterns and formations. Explore the fundamentals of technical analysis and its distinctions from fundamental analysis.

Technical analysis vs fundamental analysis

The disparity between technical and fundamental analysis is vast. While technical analysis revolves around studying past price movements, fundamental analysis considers a multitude of internal and external factors.

A fundamental analyst evaluates information to determine an asset's intrinsic value, reflecting what it would be worth if all information were priced into the market. They buy if the market price is below this value and sell if it exceeds it. For instance, when evaluating Apple shares, a fundamental analyst examines earnings reports, industry trends, and overall economic health.

In contrast, a technical analyst disregards such fundamental data and focuses solely on the asset's price chart. By employing technical indicators, they identify patterns from historical price data to forecast future price movements.

Although technical analysis may initially seem simpler, successful technical traders often utilize a wide array of indicators and rigorously test their strategies. Therefore, it's not necessarily the easier route. However, most traders opt for a combination of technical and fundamental analysis to ensure a comprehensive understanding. For instance, they might use fundamental analysis to select a market and technical analysis to time their entry into positions.

Understanding more about technical analysis

Traders can employ various methods for technical analysis, often focusing on historical price charts paired with technical indicators or oscillators. The goal is to recognize patterns aiding in optimal entry and exit points. Technical analysis typically employs candlestick charts, representing price movement within specific timeframes. Popular strategies utilize indicators like moving averages, Fibonacci retracements, and Bollinger bands, tailored to individual trading styles, markets, and timeframes.

To validate strategies, analysts often conduct back-testing, applying them to past market data before risking capital. Successful back-testing instills confidence in using technical analysis for live trades. Some traders even automate their strategies using algorithms for trade execution, minimizing human intervention.

Candlestick colors denote price movements (green for upward, red for downward), while bars indicate opening and closing prices, and wicks signify highest and lowest prices.

What is the basis of technical analysis

At the heart of technical analysis lies Dow theory, formulated by Charles Dow during the mid-19th to early 20th century. This framework outlines principles of market action, delineating trends, phases of price movements, and the influence of news on markets.

Despite advancements in technology and automation, Dow's principles remain fundamental to modern technical analysis. Key assumptions include the belief that charts convey valuable insights, enabling prediction of future movements based on historical prices. However, it's generally recommended to blend fundamental and technical analysis for comprehensive market understanding prior to trading.

Moreover, technical analysts adhere to the notion that market prices move in trends, as per Dow theory's three trend timeframes: primary movement spanning years, secondary reaction lasting from days to a year, and minor movement occurring within seconds to days. Additionally, analysts anticipate historical trends to recur, leveraging past price patterns to optimize trading decisions and maximize profits.

How is technical analysis used

Technical analysis serves both short-term and long-term trading strategies. For instance, a long-term trend investor may employ technical indicators to determine opportune moments for portfolio stock purchases, whereas a short-term day trader might utilize them to pinpoint rapid profit opportunities.

Timing plays a pivotal role in trading success, and technical analysis aids in optimizing trade execution to enhance profits and mitigate losses.

Accessible across various markets, technical analysis merely requires a price chart and access to relevant technical indicators. Thus, whether trading in forex or other markets, technical analysis proves invaluable in decision-making processes.

Limitations of technical analysis

1. Subjectivity: Technical analysis can be subjective, as different traders may interpret the same indicators differently. This subjectivity can lead to varied conclusions even when analyzing the same data.

2. Self-Fulfilling Prophecy: There's a risk of creating a self-fulfilling prophecy. When a significant number of traders act upon the same technical signals, it can reinforce the predicted price movement. However, this can also create challenges in executing trades when markets become overcrowded with similar orders.

3. Accuracy: Despite its widespread use, technical analysis is not foolproof. It's not uncommon for unexpected market movements to defy technical signals, resulting in unexpected losses for traders.

4. Ignoring Fundamentals: Technical analysis focuses solely on price movements and tends to

overlook fundamental factors that can influence market prices. Neglecting these underlying fundamentals can limit the trader's understanding of the market dynamics, leading to missed opportunities or unexpected volatility.

5. Risk Management: Traders should remain vigilant about the potential drawbacks of their technical analysis strategy and take proactive measures to mitigate risks. This may involve diversifying analysis methods, incorporating fundamental analysis, or implementing robust risk management practices to safeguard against losses.

Step 8: How to send orders and different order types in forex

Often, fluctuations in financial markets are a common occurrence throughout the trading day. Given this volatility, some traders opt for automated orders to execute trade entries or exits when a market hit predetermined price levels.

A variety of forex orders are utilized by traders to effectively manage their trades. While the specific order types available may differ among trading platforms and brokers, there are several fundamental ones that are commonly offered. Familiarizing yourself with these order types and comprehending their functionalities can enhance your trading proficiency.

In this instructional session, I will delve into the prominent types of orders and provide insights into their application within your trading endeavors.

Market orders

Market orders, as the name suggests, are executed "at market," meaning they are executed immediately at the prevailing market price. This order type is commonly utilized by scalpers and day traders who seek swift entry and exit from the forex market in alignment with their trading strategies. For instance, if you place a "buy" market order while the EUR/USD currency pair is priced at 0.86091, your order would promptly execute at the ongoing market price. This principle also applies to "sell" market orders for short positions.

Entry orders

The following most frequently used forex order type is an entry order, offering a distinct feature of being set away from current market prices.

This enables traders to initiate positions when a market's price exceeds or falls below its present level by specifying a desired entry point. Trading with entry orders offers various advantages, particularly eliminating the need for continuous market monitoring to execute trades. Typically, entry orders are employed for breakout strategies or other tactics that necessitate execution once the price surpasses a specific threshold.

Limit orders

A limit order directs your broker to execute a trade at a specific level that offers a more advantageous price than the current market rate. In forex trading, there are two types of limit orders: one to initiate a trade and the other to conclude it.

Nonetheless, there's a potential drawback wherein your order may go unfilled if your target price isn't reached within your designated timeframe. In cases where an unfilled limit order to close exists, this could result in your trade lingering in the market longer than initially planned.

Limit orders to open a trade

A limit entry order allows traders to enter the market at a more advantageous price point.

For instance, suppose the EUR/USD pair is trading at 1.21411 (as indicated in the initial deal ticket), and you anticipate it dropping to 1.1110 before rebounding. In this scenario, you would set a limit order to buy at the specified price. If the market reaches that level, your trade will be executed, opening your position at the best available price based on your designated entry point.

Similarly, for 'sell' trades, if the EUR/USD pair is trading at 1.11431 and you anticipate it rising to 1.1300 before declining, you would place a limit order to sell at 1.1200 to enter the market at that specific price. When employing a limit order, your trade will solely be executed at the price you specified or improved.

Limit orders to close a trade

You can utilize a limit order to exit a trade when the market moves a predetermined distance in your favor.

For instance, suppose you purchased EUR/USD at 1.1517 and aimed to exit when your trade exhibited a profit of 100 pips. In this scenario, you would position a 'sell' limit order 100 pips above your entry, at the 1.1618 price level.

Similarly, if you shorted EUR/USD and aimed to sell to close your position when your trade indicated a profit of 100 pips, you would follow the same process, as illustrated in the second deal ticket below.

Stop orders

Stop orders are commonly employed in forex trading as well. Similar to limit orders, there exist two variations: one stop order to initiate a trade and another to terminate it.

Stop orders to open a trade

In the dynamic world of trading, employing stop orders adds a strategic layer to your market maneuvers. Picture this: envisioning EUR/USD poised for a surge beyond the 1.11550 mark, you could set a 'buy' stop order at 1.11551. Upon breaching this threshold, your stop order seamlessly transitions into a market order, swiftly executing at the prevailing rate.

Similarly, when anticipating a downturn post the 1.11516 level in the market, crafting a 'sell' stop order at 1.11506 ensures your position opens at the opportune moment. It's all about seizing the momentum, leveraging stop orders to your advantage in navigating market breakouts.

Stop orders to close a trade

In the intricate dance of trading, employing protective stop orders emerges as a vital tool for prudent risk management. Think of it as your safeguard against adverse market movements, poised to swiftly close a trade once the market veers a predetermined distance against your position.

For instance, envision you're initiating a 'sell' trade, aiming to cap your risk at 50 pips. Placing a protective buy-stop order 50 pips beneath your entry locks in this risk threshold. The same principle applies inversely for 'buy' trades, ensuring your risk exposure remains finely calibrated amidst market fluctuations.

EUR/USD

How to place a forex order

Navigating the forex market through the intuitive trading platform is a breeze. Here's a breakdown to ensure seamless order placement, a process consistent across major platforms:

1. Access the deal ticket and locate the 'order' tab.

2. Determine the direction of your trade – whether it's a buy or sell.

3. Pinpoint your desired price level, pivotal in defining the order type based on its relation to the current market price.

4. Implement stops or limits to manage risk or lock in profits.

5. Finalize by submitting your order.

Prioritize acquainting yourself with the intricacies of your chosen platform before delving into trading activities. This proactive approach mitigates the risk of operational mishaps during trade execution or management.

Below, an illustration from an IG deal ticket highlights the price field for setting your execution level. While specifics may vary, the fundamental process remains consistent across platforms, ensuring a smooth trading experience.

NOTE: In the multifaceted realm of trading, an array of orders awaits at your disposal for entering or exiting positions. These orders aren't merely transactional tools; they serve as strategic instruments to precisely time market entry at designated prices or gracefully exit at predetermined profit thresholds. Furthermore, they function as guardians of your capital, effectively curtailing losses through astute risk management strategies. Mastering the art of order execution empowers traders to navigate the market terrain with precision and finesse, maximizing opportunities while safeguarding against potential pitfalls.

Step 9: Get to know what traders use and how the think from a professional standpoint on 'IG' platform community

Quote from Dash 1, a community member on "IG" platform, posted October 7, 2016: "I thought as a member of this fantastic community, I will share some of my experience as a trader so that new traders don't end up making the same mistakes that I have made over the years.

Firstly, I am not a professional trader however, I have been doing this on and off for a few years now. I am sure there are other members in this community that have a lot more experience and can contribute to this thread. Like I have indicated previously this thread hopefully will help new beginners in making profits.

Okay, if you are reading this then I will assume that you have an IG account. This is one of the most important aspects of trading in my opinion. Having a good broker with an excellent trading platform. I have used many platforms previously and am happy to say that IG has met all my expectations and more. I need to point out that I am not an employee of IG. The fact of the matter is they offer a fantastic platform built for mobile and web. So naturally, the first point that I would make to a new trader is to find a reputable broker.

Secondly, in keeping with the theme of brokers, ensure that they have a demo account option. Lucky for us, IG wins on that front as well.

Now that you have your account opened, and funded, you are ready to trade? Not yet... This is one of the biggest mistakes that I made when first starting out. I was so eager to trade, that I ended up losing a good portion of my initial investment. If I could turn back the hands of time, I would have spent more time reading, reading, and more reading. There is so much of free information available on the Internet and YouTube that you have no excuse to learn what in fact CFDS are and, how they work. I wish someone had told me that before I thought I knew everything…."

Posted November 21, 2016 by Dash 1: "Understanding fundamental and technical Analysis.

In today's post I wanted to share a little bit about why understanding technical and fundamental analysis is so important. As I previously mentioned, I am not an expert and I'm learning day by day however, in order to become a successful trader, you must understand why the market moves in the way it does.

Depending on which country you reside in, does a strong or weak US dollar affect your market? If so, do you know why? Is the market that you trade in heavily weighted in commodities? These are some of the crucial aspects of fundamental analysis that you need to understand before placing a trade.

Let me illustrate with an example. The South African top 40 index is heavily weighted in currency sensitive stocks. The South African market is also heavily weighted in commodities. A week South African rand and high commodity prices often drive this market higher. The same can be said about the FTSE to a certain extent.

You need to take some time out and do a little research as to why gold for example, moves the way it does.

Once you get a grip of the basics, you can then follow this up with technical analysis through the use of charts. There are plenty free resources available on the Internet with regards to how to interpret different types of charts.

Take your time and get an understanding of how candle patterns work. What is a bullish candle? What is a bearish candle? Some of you who are experienced may find this section of the post and little boring however, there are a lot of people who don't know anything about how to interpret charts."

Quote from Guest Crown boy, a community member on "IG" platform, posted May 7, 2017:

Hi, I thought I'd share my experience as a trader in BIOTECH stocks on the US exchanges. I have been trading with both cash (shares) and leverage/margin (CFD) since 2012 on/off as this is my hobby and I trade because I enjoy it. I do day, long and some short-term trading. I would say I am not a technical trader, but I do use indicators such as charts, fundamentals, investor sentiment and of course some DD (due diligence) to guide me in trades. I am not very advanced (some would say smart) as I do not do spreads and rarely trade with stops. I will try and explain why later.

So, before I start let me share some thoughts with you, some seen through the eyes of a day trader:

1. Decide what you are trading for. Is it capital gain or (additional) income? This is important as it should determine the type of trader you will be.

2. Try to focus on one market i.e. I only trade in the BIOTECH segment, but not saying I will not do a quick trade in another market. But try and focus because when you get out there it is a big world and there is money to be made in every corner, according to the market makers, fellow investors and so on. You can get defocused quiet easily, and you cannot keep up with the flow and amount of information. After all you are trying to make an informed decision on whether to enter a position or not.
3. Are you a positive (bull / long) or negative (bear / short) trader, or maybe both? For long trading either or will work fine, for day trading you probably should look into doing both because of the market mechanics (up and down). Obviously don't alternate and be a bull one day and a bear the next, but follow the market trend – here is where charts come in handy.
4. Whether you day or long trade set up a goal. How much do I want to make per day, per week

or per month. Keep in mind that even if you "only" set your goal to $100 per day it is still $100x22days=$2200 per month! And it is easy to make the $100 by doing day trading i.e. you buy 1000 shares and therefore only need a $0.1 up or down, not taking fees, taxes and so on into account. But keep in mind, the longer in the future your goal is, the higher a stock need to go up, or down for that matter. Most importantly, do not be greedy. Exit at your goal. When you become greedy you lose money. Easier said than done I know. We are humans and want to make as much as possible. No one wants to exit too early and then see a stock take off – that will leave you with a lot of regret, but so will a late exit and a big drop!

5. Many have said it before, but it is important. Never invest more than you are willing to lose in a particular trade. So again, set a goal for what you will accept in loss. You will get emotional; especially when a stock goes the wrong

direction, but never double up or down to avoid loss. Or for that matter take a reverse position, it can get very messy. Many times, you cannot salvage an investment gone bad, but will only end up with a bigger loss. Cut it loose and take the loss. Yes, I did not mention stop loss. I will explain later.

6. Trading is emotional, especially because you are trading with your own money. So, if you do a demo account first you will see you will do better than when you start trade with your own money. It is difficult to pull the trigger when it is your own money. Try and overcome that barrier. I did it by keeping track on all my trades until I became comfortable with trading (pulling the trigger). I wrote down the entry and exit point and P/L. I actually still write down my entry target price, but on a post it.

7. Plan your trade/day. Pick out your targets and do research on them, settle on an entry price and most importantly do not chase the stock if it

starts to move unexpectedly! That is when you become a bag holder. Timing is difficult in the market and sometimes you miss the boat. Learn to let it go and move on to the next stock, same as you need to learn to leave money on the table. Maybe plan on catching it on the reversal if you missed the boat the first time around: smiley wink: But remember there is a reason for why it moved, so be careful.

8. Never fall in love with a stock! Again, it is all about emotions, and there are more retail investors than ever, and most of them are emotional and in love with their stocks. So, they trade irrationally and can cause big swings in the market which some market makers take advantage of i.e. bear or bull raids.

Quote from Trev beats, a community member on "IG" platform, posted march13, 2017: "...Go to YouTube and study like crazy different strategies. Listen to IG morning call at 7.30 and 10.30 and know the price action and the price market.

When you trade without emotion, you're on the sweet spot."

Summary

In trading, various types of orders serve strategic purposes, facilitating entry into or exit from positions. These orders enable traders to enter markets at specified prices, exit at desired profit levels, and limit potential losses. Mastery of order execution empowers traders to navigate the market effectively, seizing opportunities while managing risks. This proficiency in order execution is pivotal for traders, as it allows them to maintain control over their trades and optimize their trading strategies. By understanding the different types of orders and their strategic implications, traders can confidently navigate the complexities of the market, making informed decisions to achieve their financial objectives.

Additionally, familiarity with order placement processes on trading platforms enhances efficiency and reduces the risk of errors. Overall, mastering order execution is a cornerstone of successful trading, enabling traders to capitalize on market opportunities while effectively managing risk.

www.ingramcontent.com/pod-product-compliance
Lightning Source LLC
Chambersburg PA
CBHW071212240526
45470CB00018B/1817